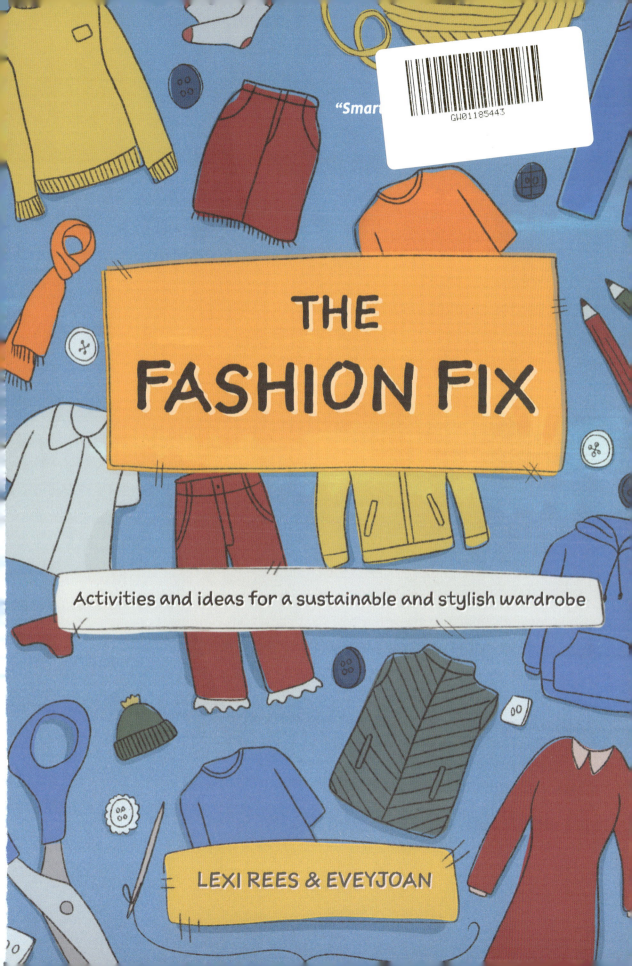

THE FASHION FIX

Activities and ideas for a sustainable and stylish wardrobe

LEXI REES & EVEYJOAN

Published in Great Britain
By Outset Publishing Ltd

First edition published July 2022

Written by Lexi Rees
Illustration and Design by Eveyjoan

Copyright © Lexi Rees & Eveyjoan 2022

Lexi Rees and Eveyjoan have asserted their rights under the Copyright, Designs and Patents Act 1988 to be identified as the authors of this work.

All rights reserved. No part of this publication may be reproduced, stored in a retrieval system, or transmitted, in any form or by any means, without the prior permission in writing of the publisher, nor be otherwise circulated in any form of binding or cover other than that in which it is published and without a similar condition including this condition being imposed on the subsequent purchaser.

ISBN: 978-1-913799-11-3

www.lexirees.co.uk
www.eveyjoan.com

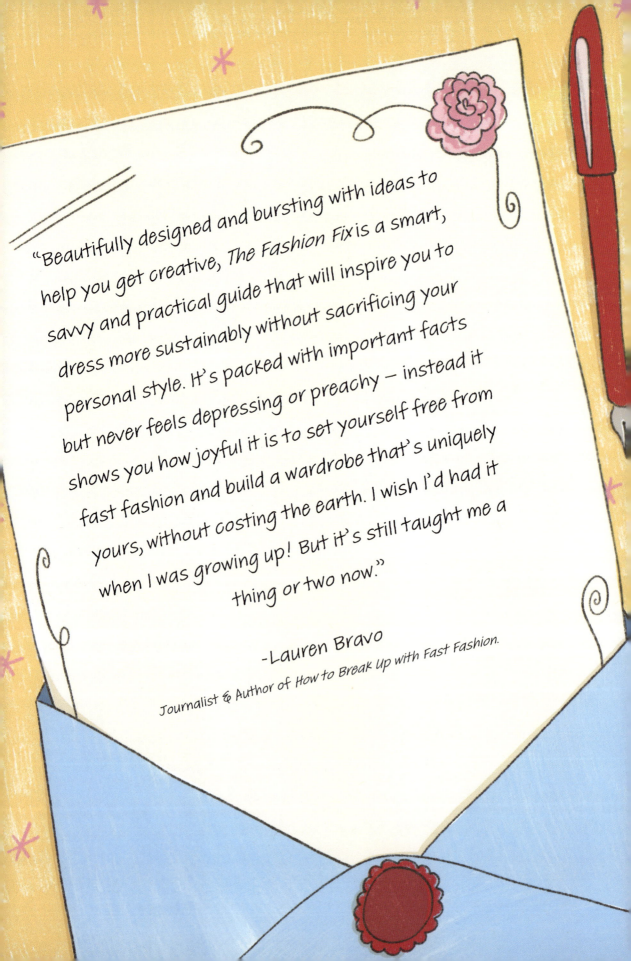

"Beautifully designed and bursting with ideas to help you get creative, The Fashion Fix is a smart, savvy and practical guide that will inspire you to dress more sustainably without sacrificing your personal style. It's packed with important facts but never feels depressing or preachy – instead it shows you how joyful it is to set yourself free from fast fashion and build a wardrobe that's uniquely yours, without costing the earth. I wish I'd had it when I was growing up! But it's still taught me a thing or two now."

-Lauren Bravo

Journalist & Author of *How to Break Up with Fast Fashion.*

CONTENTS

1. FASHION FOR GOOD

2. MATERIAL MASTER

3. RECYCLING REFRESH

4. ULTIMATE UPCYCLING

5. AGELESS ACCESSORIES

6. ECO EMBELLISHMENTS

7. IT'S COOL TO CARE

8. FIND YOUR STYLE

FAST FASHION, SERIOUS CONSEQUENCES.

Fashion is big business, but 'fast fashion' takes its toll with issues around the fashion industry's exploitation of human, animal, and natural resources.

Did you know

- We wear 20% of our wardrobe, 80% of the time.
- Most people have items in their wardrobe which have never been worn, still with tags attached.
- The average person today buys 50% more clothes and keeps them for half as long as 15 years ago.
- The average "lifetime" of an item of clothing is 2 years, and almost two-thirds of clothes end up in incinerators or landfills within a year of being made.
- Many garments are made in sweatshops with poor conditions including long hours, low wages, health and safety risks, and other violations of labour rights.
- The carbon emissions generated by the clothing of an average family is equivalent to driving a car from New York to London.
- Manufacturers use about 8,000 different synthetic chemicals to turn raw materials into textiles.
- Less than 1% of material used to produce clothing is recycled into new textiles and fibres.

Small changes to the way we dress can make a big difference to the world.

We can all practice suSTYLEability.

FASHION SEARCH

E	U	K	D	I	Y	C	M	U	R	Q	U	V	Q	G	Z	O	M	K	N
T	X	N	L	D	H	A	O	V	R	Q	R	L	M	M	N	Y	C	W	B
H	X	C	B	A	I	O	V	N	U	D	E	U	C	T	E	I	O	C	G
I	Y	Q	E	U	W	R	T	U	S	D	B	F	O	V	C	J	C	V	F
C	T	S	I	L	Y	T	S	P	O	C	C	G	G	L	A	O	Q	W	W
A	B	A	P	B	M	C	A	M	Y	T	I	L	A	N	O	S	R	E	P
L	B	X	Y	R	X	F	E	C	U	X	D	O	Z	L	G	C	E	L	C
A	S	U	S	T	A	I	N	A	B	L	E	V	U	H	H	T	N	Y	X
C	C	L	H	S	I	E	K	Y	E	A	L	G	A	S	Y	M	G	T	C
N	S	C	H	F	G	L	W	D	B	I	C	V	V	F	V	S	I	S	T
M	G	I	E	A	P	W	A	T	N	J	Y	F	F	G	K	M	S	G	D
K	O	K	M	S	B	T	D	N	V	C	C	L	O	T	H	E	S	I
N	K	I	G	R	S	E	P	K	O	B	P	U	M	L	T	F	D	M	V
Y	C	C	T	N	V	O	A	W	F	S	U	D	P	L	U	B	B	Q	E
N	M	K	K	O	S	V	R	A	B	Y	R	O	T	K	K	S	A	E	R
U	G	J	L	L	N	I	A	I	W	B	K	E	T	I	J	Y	Z	G	S
A	Z	E	Q	Q	O	W	G	D	E	T	U	T	P	R	P	I	N	P	I
A	R	T	Q	D	T	X	H	O	W	S	Q	Y	B	E	N	W	Y	U	T
P	Y	T	I	L	A	U	D	I	V	I	D	N	I	D	C	S	K	S	Y
L	M	F	Q	A	X	U	Z	P	H	X	P	S	H	O	E	Q	N	J	W

accessories
art
catwalk
clothes
colour
conscious
cool

designer
diversity
ethical
fashion
image
individuality
model

personality
preloved
style
stylist
sustainable
upcycled

LITTLE SHOP OF HORRORS

> Have you ever wondered how it can be possible for a shop to sell clothes at the very low prices we often see?

Some reasons make sense:

- Buying large quantities. The retailer can then negotiate a bulk discount to buy the garments at a lower cost.
- Buying end-of-season items. Manufacturers usually sell these at a discount so they can avoid storage costs.

But it is possible the supply chain (how a garment gets from the person who originally made it to you) has bad practices:

- Poor working conditions: long hours, no breaks, poor health and safety standards. Factories like this are called sweatshops.
- Very low pay: an hourly wage can be just a few cents.
- Child labour: an estimated 250 million children aged between 5 and 14 are forced to work in sweatshops in developing countries. And they can be working for up to 16 hours a day.

> A boycott of products from countries who use sweatshops could potentially lead to job losses and even worse working conditions. It's better to put pressure on our shops to check their supply chain.
>
> A small increase in worker wages and therefore the wholesale price (the price the retailer pays to put the item in their store) will have a minimal impact on profits for a multinational company.

Would you pay a little more for your clothes if you knew they were being manufactured responsibly?

YES/ NO

Be Brand Aware.

More and more brands have clear policies regarding the environment and social impact of their manufacturing processes and are also creating 'conscious' ranges within their collections.

Make a list of your favourite brands here and do some research to see what they offer. Check their website for policies and look at the tags in stores.

Use this list to prioritise the stores where you spend your money. The clearest way to send a message to stores that fall short, is to "vote with your feet" (or in this case, your wallet).

Store	Policy on Website?	Clear Labelling in Store?
	☐	☐
	☐	☐
	☐	☐
	☐	☐
	☐	☐
	☐	☐
	☐	☐
	☐	☐

> Did you know shopping online can have a lower environmental impact, especially if you would have driven to the store? Try to choose standard shipping instead of express shipping so the delivery company can combine orders and plan the most fuel-efficient routes.

SUSTYLEABILITY PROGRESS CHART

How sustainable is your wardrobe? Circle where you are now, and where you want to get to. Remember, it doesn't matter where you start, what you do next is what makes the difference.

1. Fashion Faux Pas

At this stage, you're shopping and dressing without being aware of the sustainability issues in your wardrobe. Don't panic! Just by picking up this book, you're already past this stage.

2. Trendsetter in Training

You recognise the choices you make about what to wear and what to buy have environmental and ethical implications and are educating yourself about suSTYLEability. Well done! This is a huge step forward. Don't forget, even if it feels a bit overwhelming as you start, just small changes can make a big difference.

3. Apparel Apprentice

You're armed with the facts and information to make the best sustainable fashion choices. Congratulations! Don't forget, if you buy an ethically manufactured, naturally dyed, organic cotton t-shirt, but then never wear it, you are not practising suSTYLEability.

4. Wardrobe Wizard

You no longer have to remind yourself to check the suSTYLEability credentials; it's become a habit. Fantastic! Don't forget to keep up-to-date on developments, like discovering new ethical brands or learning new upcycling skills.

> suSTYLEability is the only way forward for the fashion industry. You are now officially a trendsetter!

> Whatever stage of the suSTYLEability journey you're at, you can spread the word and help raise awareness.

: 2

MATERIAL MASTER

Fabric Scavenger Hunt

Can you sort the following fabrics between natural fibres and synthetics?

Have a look in your wardrobe – how many different types of fabric can you find?

Acrylic	Crepe	Lycra	Silk
Angora	Denim	Mohair	Suede
Cashmere	Fleece	Nylon	Tweed
Cotton	Lace	Polyester	Velvet
Chenille	Leather	Rayon	Viscose
Chiffon	Linen	Satin	Wool

NATURAL

MAN MADE

Plastic Fantastic

Recycling fabric is clearly good news for our natural resources, as well as reducing landfill. It's not just textiles that can be transformed.

We should try to reduce our plastic consumption, however, it's good to know plastic bottles can be turned into yarn.

There are brands which use this recycled yarn to make sneakers, leggings, fleece jackets, etc.

It takes about 9 plastic bottles to make one T-shirt.

How many brands can you find that use recycled materials to make clothes? Colour in a bottle for each brand you find.

Did you know it takes six steps to get plastic bottles ready to make into new clothes?

1. Collect the bottles. This is good news for our oceans and landfill sites.
2. Run the bottles through a sorting machine to remove anything that isn't plastic so it doesn't affect the quality of the final product.
3. Sort the bottles into different colours. Mixing colours affects the final colour of the fabric produced.
4. Chop the bottles into tiny flakes.
5. Melt the flakes down into pellets.
6. 'Extrude' the pellets, a bit like you would spin wool, stretching them into very fine string-like fibres. The fibres are tied together to create a polyester yarn.

Disastrous Denim

We all know the impact of throwaway plastics and gas-guzzling cars on the environment, but did you know denim is one of the worst offenders?

Around 2 billion pairs of jeans are made every year, using approximately 1.4 million tonnes of raw cotton.

Why is this bad?
- Cotton is a very thirsty crop.
- Growing cotton is hugely chemical-reliant.
- Even more chemicals are used to turn it into denim.

Did you know, originally the indigo colour came from a plant-based dye, but today most denim is dyed with a chemical-laden synthetic version which includes cyanide, formaldehyde and sometimes aniline?

In 2013, the pollution got so bad that the rivers in Xintang, a town in southern china which is known as the 'denim manufacturing capital of the world', turned blue.

It gets worse!

Even though we love the look, distressed denim and finishes like bleached and stone-washed cause further damage to the environment through more water wastage, quarrying for stones, and extra chemicals.

WHAT CAN WE DO?

1. Don't buy more denim than we need.

2. Upcycle vintage denim rather than throwing it out.

3. Shop at thrift stores to extend the life and reduce the carbon footprint of each pair of jeans.

4. When we buy new denim, look for more sustainable options:
   - organic cotton
   - natural indigo dye
   - less "distressed" styles as they'll have caused less distress to the planet

5. Tell our friends.

I .... do hereby commit to consciously monitoring my denim consumption.

Fur and Faux Fur

Let's talk about vintage fur.

Can the benefits of recycling and reducing landfill by not throwing the garment out compensate for the history?

....
....
....
....
....

Does wearing vintage fur create demand for new fur?

....
....
....
....
....

Do you think faux fur creates demand for real fur in the fashion industry?

....
....
....
....
....
....

How environmentally friendly is the manufacture of faux fur?

....
....
....
....
....
....

But my coat is faux fur.

LAUNDRY BASKET CHALLENGE

Sort these items into the correct laundry basket.

- cotton t-shirt
- silk scarf
- wool hat
- linen trousers
- vintage fur coat
- feather boa
- bamboo socks
- hemp bag
- jute espadrilles
- cashmere sweater

Cellulosic Fibre: This is a fibre made from cellulose, a starch-like carbohydrate which comes from plants/ vegetables.

Protein Fibre: This is a fibre taken from an animal.

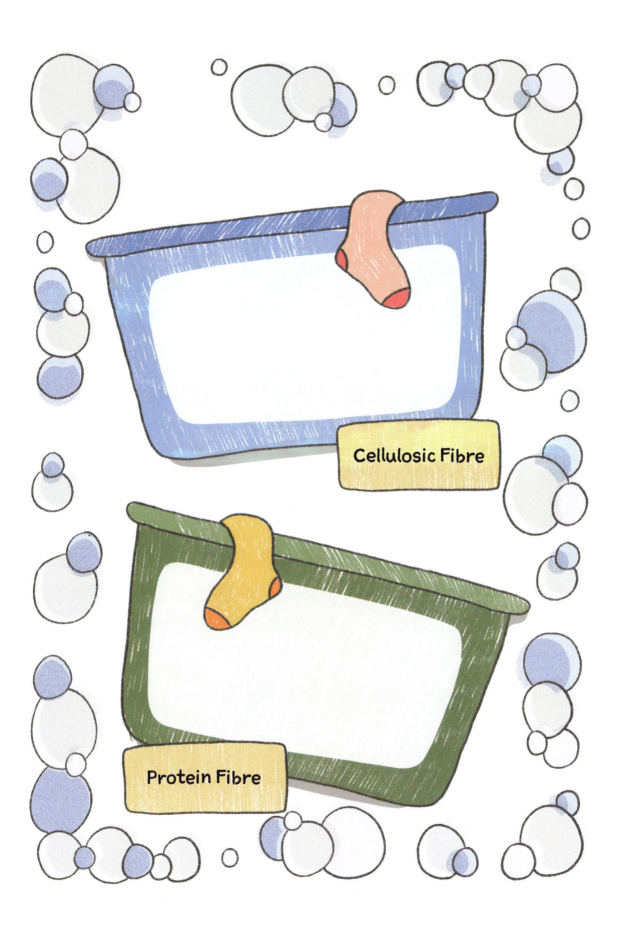

Plant Wars

We've already discovered that cotton is a very thirsty and chemical dependent plant so, although natural, we now know it has environmental issues. But what about other plant-based fibres?

BAD

Rayon is worse for the environment than cotton. Rayon was invented over 150 years ago so it's not exactly new. The problem is, whilst cotton is nice and soft to start with, rayon uses tough plant materials like bamboo and trees which are broken down through a series of chemical processes then spun into yarn using sulfuric acid. Ouch.

GOOD

Tencel is a brand name for the plant-based fibres called lyocell and modal. It feels like silk, is as breathable as cotton, moisture-wicking, durable, low-maintenance, and naturally inhibits the growth of bacteria. The production process uses chemicals which are less toxic can be recycled, so there's minimal waste. It even uses wood from trees in sustainably harvested forests. What more could you want?

Tell your friends!

Did you know bamboo yarn is a type of rayon? Manufacturers love putting "bamboo" on clothes labels as it sounds so much better than rayon. Do not be fooled!

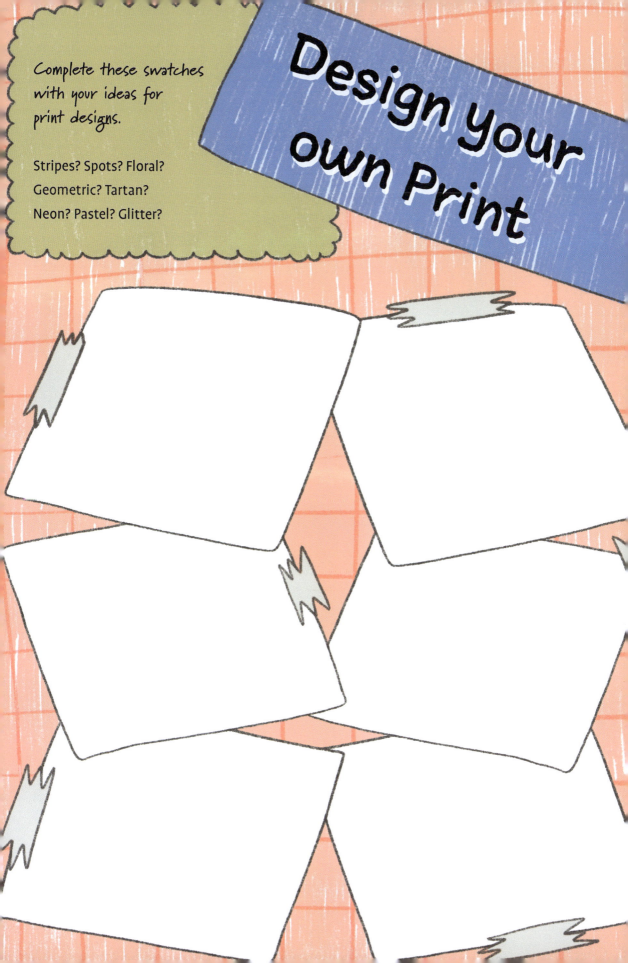

3
RECYCLING REFRESH

Pile it Up

Most of us wear 20% of our wardrobe 80% of the time!

Take everything out of your wardrobe and sort it into five piles.

1. Things I like and wear lots.

2. Things I still like but haven't worn in ages.

3. Things I don't like and never wear.

4. Things that don't fit.

5. Things that need mended or look worn out.

ONCE YOU'VE SORTED EVERYTHING, DO THE FOLLOWING.

- Put everything in pile 1 back in your wardrobe.
- Put everything in pile 2 aside. We're going to look at how we could alter or upcycle these later.
- Put everything in piles 3 and 4 in a bag ready to donate to a thrift shop and be re-loved by someone else.

- Alternatively, use them when you host a Swap Shop (see the next page for more information).
- Decide if each item in pile 5 is mendable. Even if it's beyond repair, you can still recycle the fabric so don't send it to landfill!

Multi-coloured Swap Shop

Organise a swap party with your friends.

Everyone brings clothes that they no longer want or wear.

Put all the clothes in a pile in the middle of the room.

Have fun trying on items that appeal to you.

Take home lots of fabulous pre-loved clothes.

RULES
- Only bring clothes that are clean and in good condition
- No fighting or arguments

Go large!
Set up a swap at school or for a club.

You'll need to have a system for a big event like this. Here is an example that you could use:
- drop-off garments in advance
- issue tickets (e.g. 1 ticket per item dropped off, or 3 tickets for a big/ higher value item like a coat, 1 ticket for a small item) to be exchanged as 'payment' at the swap
- set up the hall before people arrive, grouping similar items together so people can visit the jeans shop, or the dress section.

P.S. 'Multi-coloured swap shop' was a Saturday morning children's TV show that ran in the UK from 1976 to 1982 where kids phoned in and swapped toys with each other.

Don't bin leftovers – donate them to charity.

WORKS LIKE A CHARM

Most pre-loved and vintage clothes shops have racks of jewellery for sale. If you see a piece that has some nice parts, don't worry if you don't like the overall style. You can easily redesign it.

A charm bracelet is a great way to recycle your favourite finds, and you can keep adding to over time.

You will need

- assorted beads with holes
- assorted charms with hanging loops
- a piece of silver coloured chain, enough to wrap loosely around your wrist
- silver jump rings
- silver "head pins"
- wire cutters
- a lobster claw or toggle and bar clasp (bonus points if you can recycle one from another bracelet or necklace)
- pliers ('needle nose' jewellery pliers are ideal, but you can use any small ones from a regular tool kit)
- tiny "seed" beads (optional)

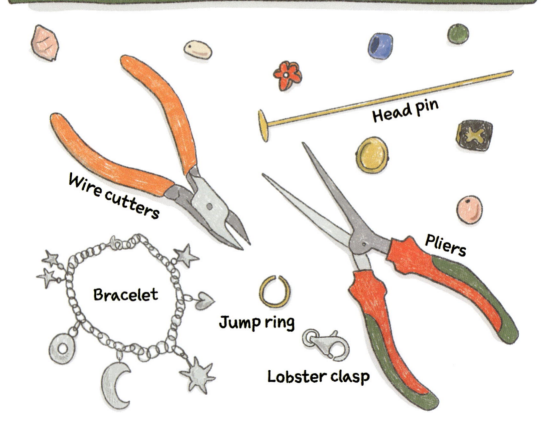

Jewellery kit is not expensive, especially when you consider how much you can save by making your own and upcycling old pieces.

Prepare your beads

1. Slip a bead onto a head pin. If the hole of the bead is too large and it just slides off the end of the pin, put a smaller bead or a seed bead on first to act as a stopper.
2. Cut the head pin to about 1 cm longer than the bead.
3. Use the pliers to bend the pin into a loop. Before you close the loop entirely, slip it through the chain and squeeze the loop together. Try to keep the loop as circular as possible. It's a bit fiddly but you'll get the hang of it after a few goes.

To finish

1. Take a jump ring for each bead or charm. Look carefully and find the join in the ring. Gently prise it open using the pliers.
2. Use the jump ring to attach the prepared bead or charm to the chain.
3. Repeat for as many beads and charms as you want to add, spreading them along the length of the chain.
4. Add the clasp to one end of the chain using a jump ring.

Punch Needle Pencil Pot

You will need

- leftover or recycled yarn in several colours. They can be different thicknesses – this adds a lovely texture to your design.
- a clean tin can
- a piece of "monks cloth" or linen, big enough to wrap around the tin can plus enough extra to fit the embroidery frame
- a felt tip pen
- a punch needle
- scissors
- PVA glue
- a rectangular embroidery frame, bigger than your pot
- needle and thread (optional)
- masking tape (optional)

Instructions

1. Draw the outline of your pot and any design you like on the cloth.

2. Put the cloth into the frame, making it as tight as possible.

3. Thread your punch needle according to the instructions.

4. Punch the needle through the fabric and carefully lift it out, keeping the tip of the needle as close to the fabric as you can.

5. Move the needle a very small way along the cloth (it doesn't need to be an exact distance). Now punch the next stitch.

6. Keep going, filling in your design as you go. Tighten the frame if the fabric comes loose.

7. When you finish, take the design out of the frame and remove any masking tape. Fold the hem over and sew or glue it down.

8. Cover the can in glue.

9. Wrap the cloth around the can, with the loopy side out, and press it down firmly onto the glue. If you want, sew the side seam up to make it extra secure.

Top tip: If you're using monks cloth, it frays like crazy. Stick masking tape on the edges while you're working to stop this.

IT'S A WRAP

'Furoshiki' is a traditional Japanese way to wrap gifts and it's awesome. This is called "furoshiki". What a great way to reuse vintage fabric, plus the fabric itself can be re-used multiple times. So much better than wrapping paper!

What fabric can I use?
Anything!

How much fabric do I need?
It depends on what you want to wrap. A rule of thumb is the fabric should be three times the size of your gift along the diagonal line.

How do I wrap a gift?
Easy! Just place your fabric onto a flat surface with the pretty side down. Put your gift in the middle of the fabric. Grab two opposite corners and knot them over the gift. Do the same with the remaining two ties.

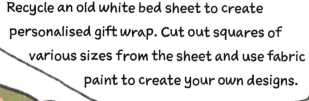

Recycle an old white bed sheet to create personalised gift wrap. Cut out squares of various sizes from the sheet and use fabric paint to create your own designs.

MAGIC FELT CUSHION

Grown out of your favourite sweater? Is it full of holes? Spotted a sweater in your favourite colour in a thrift shop but it doesn't fit? Turn them into 'boiled wool' fabric and use it to create cushions for your room.

You will need
- 100% wool sweaters
- two tennis balls
- small cushion pad
- sewing machine (optional)
- needle
- thread
- scissors

The first thing to do is check the label. This will only work if the garment is 100% wool. It might work with slightly lower wool content (to c.80%), but it's a bit hit or miss. Remember that cashmere, mohair, merino and angora are all types of wool.

Now you're going to do the exactly the opposite of the washing instructions on the label!

The hotter the water and the more you beat up the wool, the better it will felt.

Top tip: throw an old tennis ball or two into the washing machine (but not one you want to play with afterwards).

Set the machine as hot as it will go, and keep your fingers crossed. If the fabric is not completely matt when you take it out, repeat the boil wash.

Dry the shrunken garment flat.

Here are two designs to inspire you, but you can make up your own.

 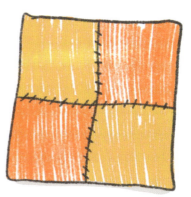

Cut out squares for the front and back (2 for a single colour cushion, 8 for a patchwork effect). The good news is, it won't fray so you don't need to hem it, but add about 3cm to the size of your cushion pad to allow for the seams.

If you're using a sewing machine, with right sides together, sew round three sides. If you're hand sewing, you could use blanket stitch and a contrasting embroidery thread.

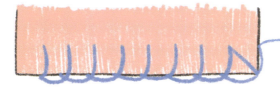

If it's inside out, turn the cushion cover the right way and poke out the corners.

Insert the cushion pad and sew up the last side.

SWEATER SLEEVE GIFT BAGS

Fine knit sweaters and cardigans make fancy gift bags for soaps, bath bombs, candles, etc.

You will need

- An old fine knit sweater or cardigan. A cuff gives the finished bag a nice extra feature but is not essential.
- Sewing machine/ needle and thread
- Scissors
- Ribbon

Instructions

1. Turn the sweater inside out and cut the sleeve off about 15cm from the end (or to fit your gift, allowing for a hem).
2. Decide if you want the arm seam to run up the side of your gift bag, or the middle of the back.
3. Once you've positioned the seam, hem the cut edge by hand or machine. Leave enough of a hem that it doesn't matter if it frays a little.
4. Turn the pouch the right way out.
5. Tie the bag with a recycled ribbon.

Shaggy Raggy Rug

Make a cosy rug to put beside your bed.

You will need
- lots of fabric remnants or old clothes. Coloured t-shirts and swimsuits are perfect.
- a piece of hessian whatever size you want your rug to be with c.5cm extra around it for the hem
- a felt tip pen
- a latch hook
- scissors
- PVA glue
- needle and thread (optional)
- anti slip mat (optional, but highly recommended, especially if the rug is going on a wooden or tiled floor)

Instructions
1. Cut the hessian to your required size. You could even make it round if you want.
2. Cut the fabric into long strips about 1.5cm wide.
3. Layer the strips about 5 deep (depending how sharp your scissors are) and cut each strip into sections about 7cm long. It doesn't matter if they are not exact.
4. Draw your design on the hessian.
5. Hold a small strip of your first fabric behind the hessian. Poke the latch hook through the hessian from the front and grab the strip. Pull half the strip through.
6. Move the hook a few holes along the hessian (it doesn't need to be exact). Poke it through, grab the other end of the fabric strip, and pull it through.
7. Keep going, filling in your design as you go. Don't forget to leave the border around the edge.
8. When you finish, turn your work over. Fold the hessian border over and sew or glue it down.

Once you master this rag technique you can get creative and make all sorts of things – festive wreaths, flower arrangements, hairbands, snuffle mats for dogs. No scrap of fabric ever needs to get wasted.

SANDWICH WRAPS

Next time you have a packed lunch, swap the foil or plastic wrap for reusable fabric wraps.

You will need

- Square of cotton, at least 14" by 14"/ 35cm x 35cm
- 1 tbsp beeswax pastilles or grated beeswax (you can buy this online)
- 0.35 oz / 10g sustainably sourced pine resin (optional, but will improve the flexibility of the finish)
- 1 tbsp. organic jojoba oil (optional, but will improve the stickiness of the finish)
- 2 press studs
- Double boiler pan, or a small saucepan and a measuring cup
- Baking tray
- Baking parchment paper
- Pinking shears (if you want a zig-zag edge), or scissors
- Paintbrush

Instructions

1. Preheat the oven to 200C or the lowest setting.
2. Cut the fabric into a square approximately 14" by 14". Pinking shears give a zig-zag edge which helps prevent the fabric from fraying, but ordinary scissors will also work.
3. Cover the baking sheet with the parchment to protect it.
4. Put the fabric on top with the patterned side down and set aside while you prepare the beeswax mixture.
5. Place the beeswax, jojoba oil, and pine resin in a double boiler or glass measuring cup and set in a saucepan. If you're just using beeswax, you can skip this stage and just sprinkle it over the fabric and pop it in the oven for about 6 minutes.
6. Add water to saucepan until it comes halfway up the measuring cup.
7. Bring the water to the boil and simmer until everything is melted together (about 20 minutes). Remove from the heat.
8. Brush the beeswax mixture onto the fabric. Make sure you go right to the edges. Don't be tempted to use too much or the finished fabric will be very thick. It's easier to add more later than take it away.
9. Put the baking tray in the oven for a few minutes to let the mixture soak into the fabric.
10. Remove the tray and leave it to cool.
11. Sew the press studs into opposite corners.
12. To use your wrap, fold it like an envelope.

Note
after use, rinse in cold water. With care, they should last 6-12 months, which is way better than single use plastic or foil.

Pinking Shears

EIGHT NO-SEW ALTERATIONS

1. Cut the sleeves and collar off an old top.

2. Cut slits into the back of a baggy t-shirt to give a cool cut-out effect.

3. Cut the hem off a pair of denim shorts to create a frayed edge look.

4. Wrap coloured embroidery threads tightly around an old belt so they completely cover it. Glue the ends onto the back of the belt.

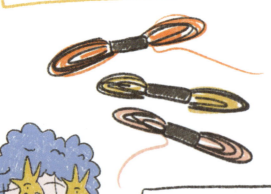

Match the thread to your favourite outfit or create a rainbow effect.

5. Cut off the hem, then cut a fringe all the way round the bottom of a t-shirt. You could even add beads to the fringe — just tie a knot to hold the bead in place.

6. Add studs to a denim jacket to give it a street look. You could put them in a line across the back from shoulder to shoulder, or freestyle.

7. Stick a row of rhinestones onto the straps of sandals or flip flops.

8. Replace boring shoelaces with ribbons.

GIVE A SWIRL A WHIRL

Tie-dying is great way to create new and totally unique designs. It's also handy if your favourite white t-shirt has gone a bit grey in the wash or has a stain you can't shift.

You will need

- a white/ pale t-shirt (100% cotton works best, avoid 100% synthetic)
- several eco-friendly fabric dyes
- 4 or 5 large elastic bands
- a plastic sheet or refuse sack (this can get messy!)
- rubber gloves
- stick/ wooden spoon

Note: you might want to do this outside to avoid accidentally dying your carpet/ sofa/ curtains/ walls...

Note: Wash your upcycled t-shirt in the machine on its own the first time just in case some of the dye runs and your other clothes change colour!

1. Soak and wring out your t-shirt, then lay it flat on the plastic sheet.

2. Put the pointy end of a stick/ wooden spoon handle in the middle of the item and twirl it round, twisting the shirt. Don't let it climb its way up the stick - keep it pretty flat. You're aiming for a pizza shape. Set the stick aside.

3. Put rubber bands round the pizza so it looks like it has been sliced into eight or ten portions.

4. Follow the dye instructions. Once you're ready, pour a different dye over each pizza slice. It's best to start with the lightest colours.

5. Turn the pizza over and put it on a clean piece of plastic (to avoid the colours blending). Repeat the colouring process over the slices.

6. Pop the pizza into a zip lock bag and seal it. Put the bag in a warm place and leave it for AT LEAST 24 HOURS! The dye needs this length of time to "prove" and allow the colours to bond with the fabric.

7. Take the t-shirt out of the bag and remove the bands. Run it under cold water. Don't panic about the colour of the water, this is normal. Keep rinsing until the water runs clear - this may take a while! Hang it up to dry.

Bleach Babe

Caution:

Bleach is toxic. Please read the label on the bottle carefully and follow the safety instructions. Do not let it get on your skin or drink it. Wear rubber gloves and use it outside or in a very well ventilated room. Wash your hands when you finish.

Although bleach is not environmentally friendly, it is still better to revive an item of clothing than throw it out.

Here are some easy ideas to try.

- Put some newspaper down and lay an old pair of jeans on it. Splatter the bleach over the surface. Leave it for 10-15 minutes.

- Use a bleach pen to draw a pattern on a dark coloured pair of leggings. You could draw flowers around the ankles or go wild and cover the whole garment.

- Tape around a pocket and use a paint brush to cover the pocket with bleach.

- Stick masking tape/ painter's tape in a zig-zag down the legs of a pair of plain coloured leggings. Spray beach on the rest. Let it dry and peel off the tape.

Don't forget to rinse your newly styled garment thoroughly with cold water and let it dry before you wear it.

CAST A SHADOW

Transform a garment by dip-dying the bottom to create an "ombre" effect.

You will need

- a pale coloured item of clothing (100% cotton is best)
- eco-friendly fabric dye
- a rail to hang the item from, like a broom handle balanced between two chairs
- a bucket
- plastic bag
- elastic band
- rubber gloves

Instructions

1. Wash the garment and leave damp.
2. In a washing bowl, mix the dye with water and salt according to pack instructions.
3. Decide how far up the garment you want the dye to go. Put the bit that is to stay white into a plastic bag and tie an elastic band around it to keep it clean.
4. Submerge the rest of the garment into the dye to that level. Leave for 10 minutes. Hang the garment from your rail over the bowl with dye in it.
5. Pull the fabric out a few centimetres, then leave for another 10 minutes.
6. Continue pulling the fabric out a little every 10 minutes.
7. When you've finished dying the fabric, rinse in cold water and leave to dry on a rack.

> Next time you're giving your bedroom a makeover, consider giving your curtains a new look with an ombre effect at the bottom. This will only work if your existing curtains are pale curtains. Don't forget to ask for permission first!

Bring on the Sparkle

Sewing sequins onto the collar gives so many options for restyling a shirt.

You will need
- × A shirt with a collar
- × Sequins in your chosen sizes and colours (preferably not plastic)
- × Needle and thread

This looks amazing if you just cover the pointed tips of the collar and use different sizes of sequins.

AGELESS ACCESSORIES

ACCESSORY AUDIT

Accessory (noun)
A thing which can be added to something else in order to make it more useful, versatile, or attractive.

As accessories are often small, it's easy to lose them at the back of a drawer. On the other hand, if you leave them on display, your room can get very messy. Keep a list of all your accessories so you don't forget about them, even when they're out of sight!

ITEM	COLOUR	DESCRIPTION
Belt	Black	Patent leather, skinny

Use accessories as a cheap way to create different looks from one outfit.

Check this list before you go shopping so you don't buy duplicates. This will help you to consume less.

SCARF MAGIC

Turn a large square scarf into a glamorous summer top.

Turn a square scarf into a turban-style headwrap.

Pom-Pom Earrings

You will need
- yarn
- a pom-pom maker, or two circles cut from a cardboard box, or a fork
- scissors
- embroidery needle
- earring posts

Pom-pom gadget method:

1. Follow the manufacturer instructions.

Cardboard circles method:

1. Put the two circles together. Cut through one side of each ring as shown. Make sure the slits are lined up.
2. Start winding the yarn round the circles, sliding the yarn through the slit each time. This is quicker than feeding it through the middle, and we like speedy pom-poms!
3. Keep going until the centre is full. The more winds you do, the fluffier the pom-pom will be. Don't worry if there is a little gap at the slit, you won't see it in the finished pom-pom. Cut the yarn off.
4. Slide a pair of scissors between the two circles and snip the threads. Don't pull the circles apart yet or the pom-pom will disintegrate.
5. Take a length of yarn and slide it between the two circles. Pull it very tight and tie in a knot. Leave the tails long. It is now safe to remove the cardboard circles.

Fork method:

1. Start winding the yarn round the outside of the fork.
2. Keep going until the fork is full. The more winds you do, the fluffier the pom-pom will be. Snip the yarn off.
3. Cut a length of yarn and thread it onto an embroidery needle. Push the needle under the yarn between the central prongs of the fork. Remove the needle and wrap the yarn around the outside of bundle twice, pull it very tight and tie in a knot. Leave the tails long.
4. Now snip the yarn on each side of the fork prongs.

To finish, all methods:

1. Gently fluff your pom-pom. For extra floof, put your pom-pom in a sieve above a pan of boiling water and the fibres will separate. This works best if you're using pure wool.
2. If there are any straggly bits sticking out of your finished pom-pom you can trim them but leave the tie tails so you can attach your pom-pom to the earring.

Trace this template to make a small pom-pom or draw your own.

Make several so you can match them to your outfit.

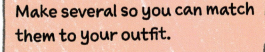

Unravel old scarves or chunky sweaters and recycle the yarn to make your pom poms.

Belt Up

Belts can be functional or part of your school uniform, but they are also a versatile accessory, can transform/ update a look, rarely go out of fashion, and last a long time.

As well as a classic black/ brown belt, look out for these styles to add to your collection:

- skinny, in lots of different colours
- wide, to cinch a waist or sling low around your hips
- braided, to create a boho chic look
- statement, to add some sparkle to a plain outfit
- long, thin silky scarves, patterned or plain

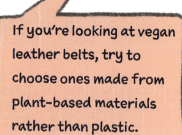

If you're looking at vegan leather belts, try to choose ones made from plant-based materials rather than plastic.

THRIFT STORE

Try putting a belt over a jacket or coat to change your silhouette

Choose three garments from your wardrobe that you have never worn with a belt and draw how you could change the look by adding a belt.

SHRINKY DINK KEYCHAIN

This is a fun way to turn plastic waste into a useful keychain.

Materials
- Plastic (not foil) crisp packet
- A key ring
- Hole punch
- Baking tray
- Foil

Instructions

Ask an adult for help using an oven.

1. Eat the crisps.
2. Preheat the oven to 250oC.
3. Wash your empty crisp packet and leave it to dry.
4. Punch a hole in the top corner of the packet.
5. Cover the bottom of a baking tray with foil.
6. Lay the crisp packet on the foil and put the baking tray in the oven.
7. Leave the crisp packet for two to three minutes. It will now have shrunk.
8. Take the baking tray out of the oven and leave your mini crisp packet to cool.

Not only have you made something useful, but you've also saved a plastic packet from going to landfill.

How creative can you get?

- Instead of punching a hole at the top corner, wait until the packet is shrunk and cooled, then glue a safety pin on the back to make a brooch.
- Cut the packet into a flower shape before you shrink it and punch the hole in one of the "petals" to make a quirky pendant.
- Punch holes in the top and bottom before shrinking and string several packets together to make a bracelet.

The Science

Plastic crisp packets are made from long chains of molecules called 'polymers'. In crisp packets, these polymer chains are straight. When you heat them up, the polymer chains get more energy which makes them vibrate and curl up over each other.

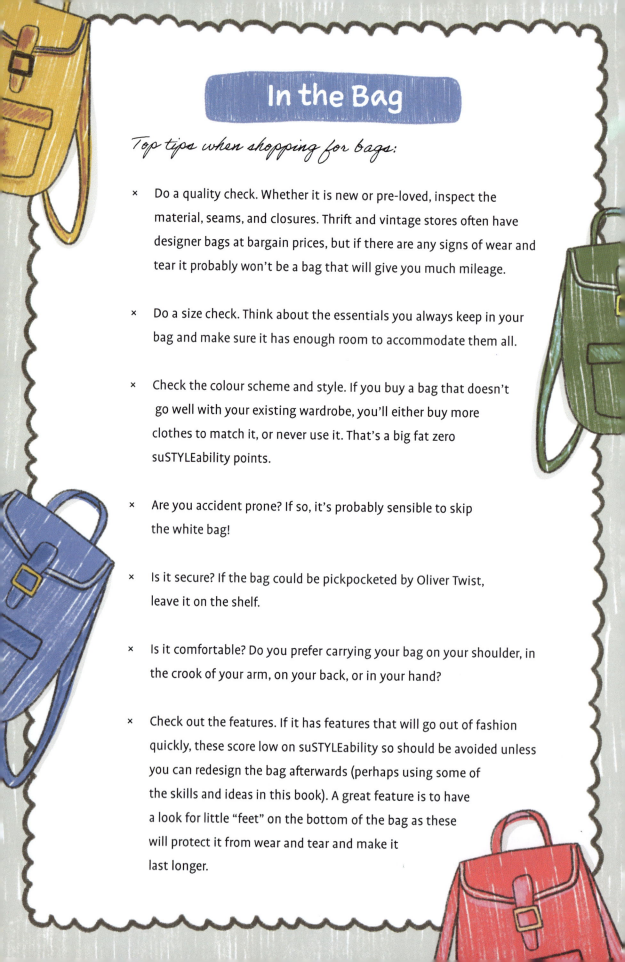

In the Bag

Top tips when shopping for bags:

- Do a quality check. Whether it is new or pre-loved, inspect the material, seams, and closures. Thrift and vintage stores often have designer bags at bargain prices, but if there are any signs of wear and tear it probably won't be a bag that will give you much mileage.

- Do a size check. Think about the essentials you always keep in your bag and make sure it has enough room to accommodate them all.

- Check the colour scheme and style. If you buy a bag that doesn't go well with your existing wardrobe, you'll either buy more clothes to match it, or never use it. That's a big fat zero suSTYLEability points.

- Are you accident prone? If so, it's probably sensible to skip the white bag!

- Is it secure? If the bag could be pickpocketed by Oliver Twist, leave it on the shelf.

- Is it comfortable? Do you prefer carrying your bag on your shoulder, in the crook of your arm, on your back, or in your hand?

- Check out the features. If it has features that will go out of fashion quickly, these score low on suSTYLEability so should be avoided unless you can redesign the bag afterwards (perhaps using some of the skills and ideas in this book). A great feature is to have a look for little "feet" on the bottom of the bag as these will protect it from wear and tear and make it last longer.

MINI BOBBLE HAT GARLAND

Just like personal stylists use accessories to transform the look of an outfit, interior designers use accessories to transform the look of a room.

You will need
- several colours of leftover or recycled yarn in wintery colours
- an empty toilet roll tube
- cotton wool balls
- a ribbon the length you want your garland to be

Instructions

1. Cut the tube into 1cm pieces.
2. Wrap the yarn around a small book 30 times, then cut along one side of the book to make 30 strands.
3. Fold a strand in half, wrap it around the section tube and pull the ends through the loop.
4. Keep going until you've covered all the cardboard.
5. Push all the ends up through the middle of the tube (this gives a 'brim' effect to the bobble hat).
6. Push the cotton wool ball inside the tube.
7. Cut another strand of yarn and tie a knot near the top of the strands to form the body of the hat and a tufty pom-pom. Trim the pom-pom to shape.
8. Repeat until you have enough to make a garland.
9. Take your ribbon and knot it round the pom-poms, spacing them out to about every 10cm.

Furoshiki Bags

In an earlier chapter, we looked at **furoshiki gift wrapping** but you can also make fabulous furoshiki bags. All you need is a very large square of fabric (the bigger the square, the bigger the bag), and your choice of handle.

There are lots of videos on YouTube which show you how to tie the bags, but it doesn't really matter as long as the knot is secure!

Here are some design ideas.

There are traditionally ten different sizes of furoshiki cloth. Each size has a different name.

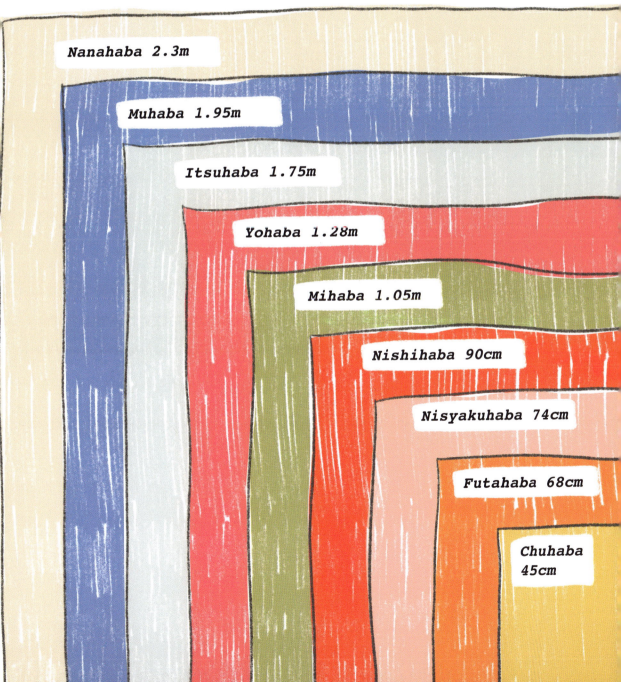

Nanahaba 2.3m
Muhaba 1.95m
Itsuhaba 1.75m
Yohaba 1.28m
Mihaba 1.05m
Nishihaba 90cm
Nisyakuhaba 74cm
Futahaba 68cm
Chuhaba 45cm

6

ECO EMBELLISHMENTS

ALL BUTTONED UP

Changing the buttons can transform an item of clothing from meh to wow.

You can buy buttons from a specialist haberdasher or there is often a haberdashery section in large department stores.

Make sure your new buttons are about the same size as the original ones or they won't fit through the buttonhole!

Save nice buttons from old items of clothing to reuse.

PEEK-A-BOO

Sew a piece of lace behind a rip in your jeans.

You will need

- Lace (stretchy lace is most comfortable)
- Needle and thread

Instructions

- Cut the lace so it is about 1cm bigger than the rip all round.
- Turn your jeans inside out and sew around the outside of the hole. Try to pick up only a few threads from the jeans fabric so the stitching doesn't show through on the other side.

This is handy if a rip in your jeans is growing and maybe exposing more leg than you want. Or if you're getting cold — you can always unpick it next summer!

A Dot and a Dash

Use simple embroidery to personalise a plain item of clothing.

Start by adding a small design to the pocket on your jeans or a shirt, and once you get more confident you can make the patterns bigger and more complex. There are lots of different embroidery stitches which will give you different textures and effects.

You will need

- embroidery thread in your chosen colour(s)
- an embroidery needle
- scissors
- tracing paper
- pins

Instructions

1. Draw your design onto the tracing paper.
2. Cut out the design, leaving a thick border around the pattern.
3. Pin the tracing paper onto the clothes where you want the design to go.
4. Cut a long piece of thread, and thread your needle.
5. Pull the thread so the needle is halfway along the thread and tie a double knot at the end.
6. Starting on the underside of the clothes, poke the needle up through the fabric and tracing paper then pull it through, checking the knot sits neatly at the back.
7. Use either running stitch or back stitch to follow the outline of your design.
8. When you finish, tie the thread at the back with a double knot and snip the loose ends off.

Embroidery Needle

Embroidery Thread

Running Stitch: push the needle through one side and then back through the other side, leaving a tiny space in between each stitch. This leaves a slightly dotted line.

Back Stitch: Start with one simple running stitch. Leave a gap the same length as the first stitch. Bring the needle up at the far end of the gap, then go backward putting the needle down through the tracing paper and fabric exactly where the first stitch finished. This gives a nice solid line and is ideal to keep your design crisp.

You can use these templates or draw your own.

JUST BEAD IT

This must be the easiest way to jazz up an old pair of shoes or sneakers.

You will need

- Two large decorative beads with wide holes
- Shoelaces

Instructions

1. Unlace your shoes.
2. Thread a single bead onto each shoelace and push it to the middle.
3. Now lace the shoes back up keeping the bead at the bottom.

LACE TRIM

Sew a lace trim onto the hem of a top.

You will need

- Enough lace to go round the bottom of the garment
- Needle and thread
- Pins

Instructions

1. Turn the top inside out.
2. Pin the lace trim along the hem, making the join at a side seam.
3. Sew along the edge. Try to only pick up a few threads from the fabric of your top so the stitching doesn't show through.

This is a good trick if you've grown and still want to wear your favourite top.

CHARM-ING

These cute charms are easy to attach to your belt loops, a jacket zipper, or a bag.

You will need
- about four chunky beads/ charms
- a piece of chunky silver chain about 5cm long
- silver jump rings
- silver head pins
- a silver keyring/ charm clip
- jewellery pliers (flat nose are great for opening the jump rings, and round nose are easiest to form the loops)
- wire cutter

Instructions

1. Insert a head pin through each charm/ bead. Snip off the excess pin, leaving about 1cm sticking out.

2. Use pliers to bend the top of the pin into a loop. Before you completely close each loop, attach the charm along the chain. About four charms on the chain works well, but you can add more or fewer if you want.

3. Use pliers to open the jump ring and slip the end of a segment of chain and the keyring into the jump ring. Use pliers to close the jump ring back into a circle.

Jump ring

Head pin

Note: jewellery kit is not expensive, especially when you consider how much you can save by making your own jewellery/ up cycling old pieces.

Use recycled beads and charms from broken jewellery.

Make several in different colours to match your outfits.

PICK-YOUR-OWN PRINT

Add a pattern to a plain, pale-coloured item of clothing such as a white t-shirt using fabric paint. This is quick and easy to achieve if you use a stamp.

You will need

- a printing stamp, or make your own by cutting your design into half a raw potato
- fabric paint
- cardboard
- sponge

Instructions

1. Lay a piece of cardboard between the fabric layers to prevent any colour seeping through.
2. Use a sponge to transfer the paint onto your stamp. This gives a more even coverage than dipping the stamp directly into the paint.
3. Press the stamp firmly down onto the fabric, hold it still while you count to three, then lift it straight up. Don't wiggle the stamp or you will smudge the design.
4. Allow the design to dry for twelve hours then iron on the reverse of the fabric to 'set' the paint. This means you can wash the clothes without damaging your design. No smelly clothes here!

You can use these templates or draw your own.

POM-POM ADDICT

Is it possible to be addicted to pom-poms?
As well as adding them to hats and scarves, why not jazz up old blankets and cushions?

Blanket-pom

See the instructions in Chapter 5 for three different ways to make a pom-pom. This time, we're going to want to use a bigger size than when we made earrings.

Choose a yarn colour that matches or contrasts with your cushion or blanket. Use the pom-pom tail to sew it onto the blanket.

Cushion-pom

Sew a strip of mini-poms onto the edge of a cushion.

Make sure you tuck the trim over at the end so it doesn't fray and you get a neat edge.

IT'S COOL TO CARE

LABEL BINGO

Now you have a carefully curated wardrobe, it's important to know how to look after it. Can you find the following washing/ care symbols on your clothes?

Machine drying your clothes massively increases the carbon impact of doing laundry. Try to air dry them instead.

A Stitch in Time

Here are seven simple repairs and alterations everyone should be able to do. Tick the ones you know how to do.

- ☐ Remove bobbles from a sweater to make it look like new again. You can get gadgets to do this, or carefully cut them off with small scissors.

- ☐ Remove annoying pet hairs from clothes. A clothes brush will work magic here, but if you don't have one, wipe the garment with a piece of sticky tape!

- ☐ Fix pulled threads in knits. Gently stretch the knit and attempt to reposition the pulled yarn. If there is still a bit extra, carefully pull the loose thread to the wrong side of the garment so it can't be seen.

- ☐ Replace a missing button.

- ☐ Move a button to make a collar or waist band fit better.

- ☐ Let down the hem on your trousers when you grow taller. When you alter a hem, you can either sew it up or use iron-on tape.

- ☐ Shorten a dress or skirt when fashions change.

- ☐ Use a patch to mend a hole.

> If your garment has a hole, you can cut it into a cool shape and turn it into a feature.

Dirty Dry Cleaning

Dry cleaning is neither dry nor clean. It is not a "dry" process as the clothes are soaked in liquid solvent. And it is not "clean" as the chemicals used are bad for the health of the person cleaning your clothes as well as for the environment.

A circle means the garment can be dry cleaned. If there's a letter inside the circle, it's to tell the dry cleaner which chemical wash and method to use.

Imagine you purchase the most sustainable garment made with organic cotton and natural dyes, sustainably manufactured, and hand-crafted by an artisan who receives fair wages, but it comes with a label that says Dry Clean Only. Are you really making a sustainable purchase?

Check the label to see if it says 'dry clean only' before buying any garment.

HANG ON!

Looking after your clothes will make them last longer.
If you have boring or mismatched clothes hangers, here is an easy way to decorate them.

Materials

- clothes hangers
- washi craft tape in a variety of colours/patterns.

Instructions

1. Starting at the tip of the hook, wrap the washi tape around the hanger, overlapping the tape slightly with each wrap.
2. Keep going all the way round.
3. Done!

Washi tape is totally recyclable and gets the Fashion Fix stamp of approval.

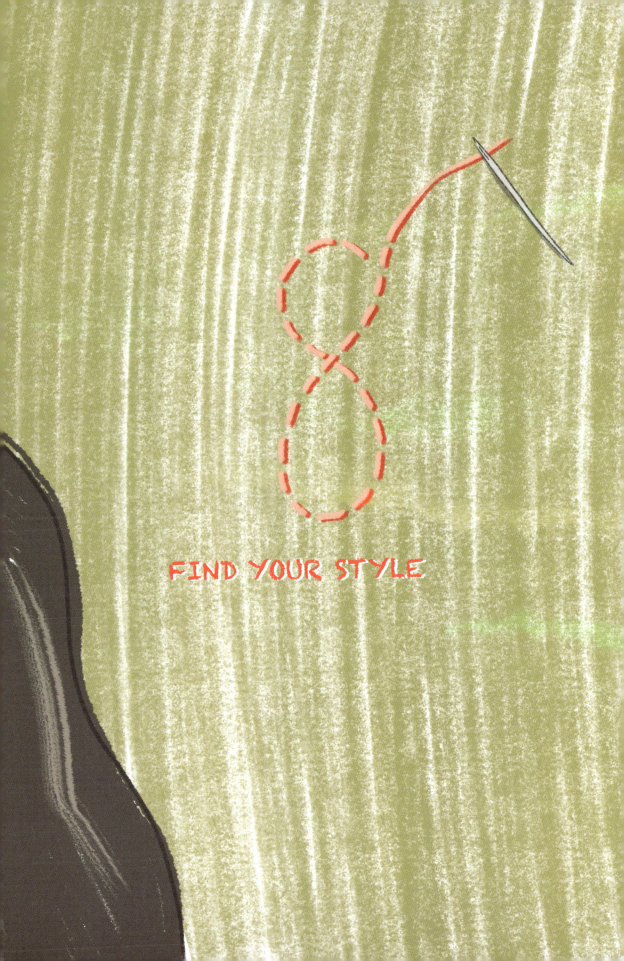

PERSONAL STYLE QUIZ

Find out what style suits your personality.

1. Which words best describe you?

A. Elegant, sophisticated, organised.
B. Friendly, casual, sporty.
C. Dreamer, kind, sensitive.
D. Brave, bold, adventurous.
E. Creative, laid-back, unconventional.

2. Which outfit you would choose?

A. Jeans, long cardigan with matching skinny belt, and a pair of ankle boots.
B. Shorts, simple top, sneakers, and small stud earrings.
C. Long floaty dress, dangly earrings, a charm bracelet, and a pair of sequined sandals.
D. Leather jacket, leggings, tunic top or dress, chunky boots.
E. Patterned top, cowboy boots, fancy belt.

3. What type of footwear do you like best?

A. Ballerina pumps.
B. Canvas sneakers.
C. Espadrilles or anything with florals or lace.
D. Flat ankle boots with studs.
E. Slouchy knee-high boots.

4. Which gift would you like to receive most?

A. A simple gold or silver necklace.
B. A baseball cap.
C. A floaty scarf in a flowery print.
D. A metal-studded belt.
E. A bright, chunky cuff.

5. Which scent would you prefer to wear?

A. Refreshing and sea salty.
B. You like to wear your own scent!
C. Fresh and floral.
D. Rich and spicy.
E. Zingy and fruity.

6. What would you wear on a beach?

A. Shorts, floaty top, canvas bag, gladiator sandals.
B. Sports bikini, sun visor, sneakers.
C. Floaty maxi dress, embellished fabric bag, strappy sandals.
D. Crop top, denim skirt, bare feet.
E. One-piece swimsuit, sarong, string bag, flip flops.

Tally your answers here:

A. 2   B. 2   C. 2   D. 2   E. .....   F. .....

YOUR STYLE ANALYSIS

Mostly As *The Designer*

Your elegant style reflects your wonderful poise and confidence. Your dream wardrobe is full of timeless pieces, and you recognise the importance of quality over quantity.

From a suSTYLEability perspective, your wardrobe will never date, reducing your clothing footprint on the planet. And because your garments are simple and classic, it's easy to use accessories to completely transform each outfit. The activities in this book should give you lots of ideas on how to have more fun with accessories.

Mostly Bs *The Champion*

Your casual and sporty style reflects your endless energy. Not only is it comfortable and practical, but it's ready to tackle life head-on.

From a suSTYLEability perspective, your look is a winner as it never follows the flashy trends of fast fashion. The activities in this book should show you how to add even more zest and zing to your sporty style.

Mostly Cs *The Visionary*

Your romantic style reflects your deep passion. Whatever inspires you – animal welfare, human rights, the environment – you have the power to make the world a better place. Go for it!

From a suSTYLEability perspective, the activities in this book should inspire you to create a wardrobe that aligns with your core values and personal ethics.

Mostly Ds *The Adventurer*

Your bold style is as strong as you are. Some might describe your look as a bit grungy but you prefer that to girly.

From a suSTYLEability perspective, the activities in this book should inspire you to create a unique wardrobe ready for every adventure and challenge you take on.

Mostly Es: *The Creator*

Your quirky style highlights your amazing individuality and creativity. You can create something unconventional from the traditional "high-street" look by adding your own unique twist. You're not afraid to try new designs, play with colour, try unusual shapes and silhouettes, and wear bold prints that make you stand out from the crowd.

From a suSTYLEability perspective, the activities in this book should inspire you to explore your unique style and help you reinvent your wardrobe multiple times.

Take Stock

Take everything out of your wardrobe and sort it into piles of similar items. How many of each do you have?

T-shirts	
Shirts	
Jackets	
Sweatshirts	
Sweaters	
Cardigans	
Jeans	
Trousers	
Leggings	
Sweatpants	
Shorts	
Skirts	
Dresses	

What garment do you have most of?

_____

If you have lots of very similar items (be honest here!), these might be your go-to comfort buys. Break the habit! Next time you find yourself reaching for one of these when you're shopping, ask yourself if you really need it. You probably don't.

Think before you buy and be a suSTYLEability superstar!

TIME TALLY

What do you think defines "good value" when you buy an item of clothing?
....
....

Make a note of what an item of clothing cost.
Keep a tally of how often you wear it.

Item	Cost	Number of times worn	Average cost per wear*

*the cost divided by number of times worn.

Being a conscious shopper means you should only buy things that you really need or will love and wear regularly. If you have a special event, consider hiring an outfit rather than buying something you will only wear once.

Better quality/ classic items may cost more to start with, but if they last longer/ don't go out of fashion so quickly then the 'cost-per-wear' may lower.

OUTFIT PLANNER

Each item you own should work with several other garments to earn its space in your wardrobe.

Pick an item from a category. Can you make four different looks with it using other garments you already own? Draw them below.

A jacket

A pair of shorts

You can apply this 'rule of four' when shopping. If an item doesn't work with four things you already own, is it a good idea to buy it?

A top

Planning different outfits in advance can help you avoid the trap of wearing 20% of your wardrobe, 80% of the time.

COLOUR CHALLENGE

How many outfits can you create from your existing wardrobe to match these styles? Don't forget to include shoes and other accessories.

Draw them in these boxes.

BRIGHT

COLOUR BLOCK

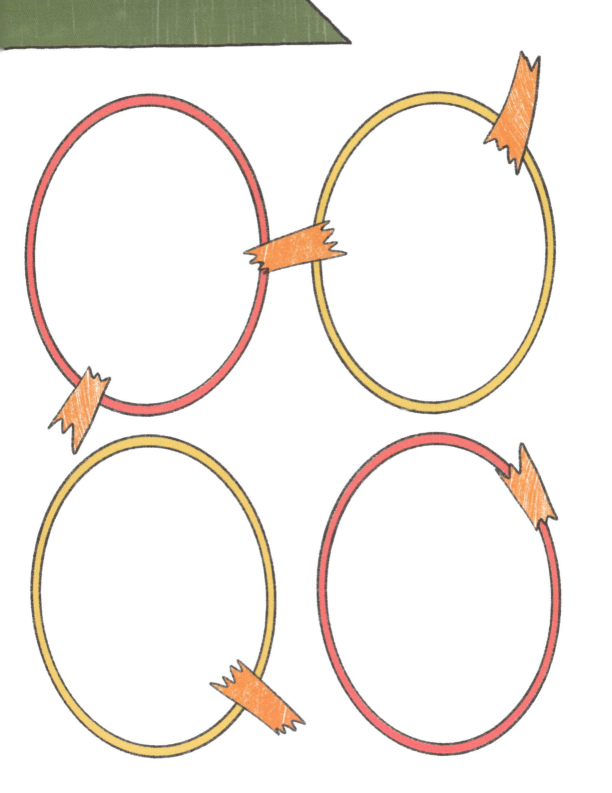

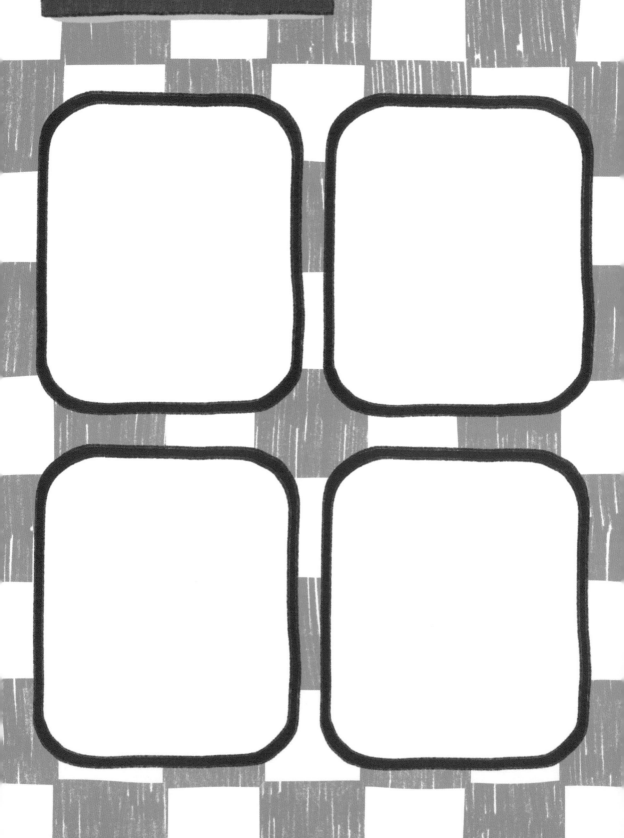

Colour Match Quiz

Buying clothes in colours that suit you can help you avoid expensive mistakes. Also, shopping within a colour palette means your clothes can be mix-and-matched more easily.

People often describe their "best" colours as the seasons.

SPRING
- Warm colours like cream, peach, golden-yellow and light orange
- Colours that are light and bright like lime green, lemon yellow, coral

Think: light and bright

SUMMER
- Light and cool colours
- Pastels and soft neutrals with pink and blue undertones
- Calm colours like sky blue, powder pink, and pale grey

Think: pale and calm

AUTUMN
- Colours with golden undertones, like camel, beige, orange, gold, and chocolate brown
- Warm shades of browns and reds
- Muted colours like rust, mustard, olive

Think: rich and spicy

WINTER
- Sharp and clear colours
- Pure white, black, blue, red, and bright pink
- Icy tones rather than pastels for the lighter colours

Think: Strong and crisp

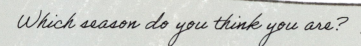

Which season do you think you are? ....

There are quizzes you can do online to determine your "season", but these can be biased by your preferences e.g. Do you like gold or silver jewellery? If you want a proper test, you need to hold lots of different colours up to your face and be honest about whether they really suit you, rather than just being colours you like. Try it! You might be surprised by the answer.

ABOUT THE AUTHOR

Lexi was born in Edinburgh and grew up in the Scottish Highlands, although she now lives down south. When she's not writing or tutoring, she's a keen crafter and spends a considerable amount of time trying not to fall off horses or boats. She's usually covered in sand, straw, or glitter.

ABOUT THE ILLUSTRATOR

Eve is a London-based illustrator and digital designer. Her quirky, creative style is characterised by bold colours and lively lines. Eve's unique background as a tattooist means her work spans from print, to digital, to people - and her ethos of sustainability is significant throughout her work and is echoed by her love of slow fashion.

ALSO BY THE AUTHOR

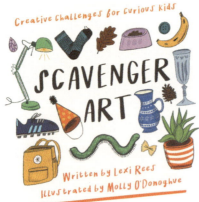
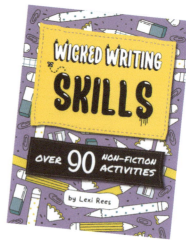
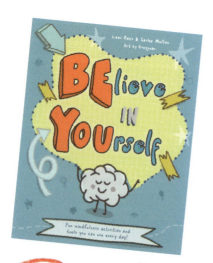
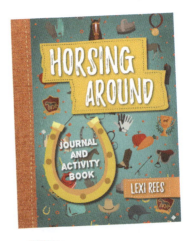

Printed in Great Britain
by Amazon